GutBuste...

LOW-FAT BARBE...

GW00420229

GutBusters started in the early 1990s with the NSW Health Department in Newcastle, Australia, in response to the growing interest among men keen to get rid of a health problem they couldn't hide—their gut. In 1995, the `at-home' program became available and during the next 3–4 years, over 50 000 men took on the challenge.

It became obvious that *real* men are interested in *real* food. Once they start to see less of themselves, there is a desire to go even further—not only to eat more interesting food but also to try their skills in the kitchen.

This is a cookbook guaranteed not to intimidate the novice cook, yet with recipes to excite even the more accomplished chef. From the perfect steak with coleslaw to chargrilled salmon with balsamic marinade—all the recipes have been designed to make sure that while you fill up, you won't fill out.

Other GutBuster titles

GutBuster Waist Loss Guide
GutBuster 2: The High Energy Guide
GutBuster Recipes
GutBuster: Low-Fat Snacks & Sweets

GUTBUSTER

LOW-FAT BARBECUES

Recipes for men

Garry Egger

Recipes by Julie Albrecht

Cartoons by Sue Plater
and Garry Egger

ALLEN & UNWIN

First published in 1999
Allen & Unwin
9 Atchison Street
St Leonards NSW 1590
Australia
Phone: (61 2) 8425 0100
Fax: (61 2) 9906 2218
E-mail: frontdesk@allen-unwin.com.au
Web: http://www.allen-unwin.com.au

National Library of Australia
Cataloguing-in-Publication entry:

Egger, Garry.
GutBuster low-fat barbecues: recipes for men.

ISBN 1 86508 102 7.

1. Barbecue cookery. 2. Low-fat diet—Recipes. I. Plater, Sue.
II. Albrecht, Julie. III. Title.

641.76

Set in Palatino and Futura by DOCUPRO, Sydney
Printed and bound by McPhersons Printing Group, Maryborough, Vic.

CONTENTS

Side dishes

INTRODUCTION

This is the first in a series of planned recipe books for men from the GutBuster program. And let's be honest, this one's a bit of a steal. The idea came from an Aussie BBQ book which I picked up in a newsagency on Thursday Island one lazy Saturday afternoon in between busting guts in the Torres Strait. It was a great idea. It had great cartoons. But the menus! They looked like they'd been put together by the two fat ladies during a binge. There was enough fat in the first couple of pages to make any greasy chip lover think he had died and gone to heaven.

Anyway, never one to pass up someone else's good idea, I decided to add the notion of BBQs to the list of recipe books we planned for men. To enable the bellies of the world to unite (perish the thought), I enlisted my long-time cartooning partner, Suzie ('Seafood') Plater, and Gold Coast nutritionist Julie Albrecht. Suzie has been the pen behind my scattered thoughts for over 15 years. She is also the pen behind the GutBuster logo on the front cover, which has been so good to us since 1991, and the cartoonist for all the GutBuster books and literature.

Julie Albrecht has busted guts with me on several occasions, including courses with GPs and with indigenous men in the Torres Strait. As a fully qualified nutritionist, Julie is ideally suited to the task. As you'll see, her recipes are about the tastiest you'll find to 'waist away' while gathered around the backyard institution. In line with the GutBuster program, we've also included fat scores (in grams) for each recipe. The general idea is to try to keep daily fat intake down below 40 g and to avoid any foods that are higher than 10% fat. You'll find all these recipes fit both categories.

GutBusters started in the early 1990s with the NSW Health Department in Newcastle, Australia, amid a flurry of interest from men who wanted to get rid of a health problem they couldn't hide—their gut. Many more hid around corners and watched the progress of those bold enough to 'come out' and attend a course in 'waist reduction'. It wasn't until the 'at-home' program was offered in 1995 that they started coming out of the woodwork—over 50 000 of them over the next 3 or 4 years.

As part of this process, it became obvious that real men are really interested in real food. Once they start to see less of themselves, there's a desire to go even further; to taste flavours they've never tasted and feel energy they thought they could only ever recover by being gelded.

Our first *GutBuster Recipes*, by nutritionist Rosemary Stanton, was (and still is) a runaway success. So we decided to do some more. This time though, we thought we'd change the format to suit men more. Hence the pocket book-sized editions, with cartoons to lighten the load, and liberal sprinklings of 'waist-whittling' tips. This is the first in the series. But several others are on the drawing boards. We hope you'll enjoy the taste of these GutBuster BBQs without suffering the abdominal consequences of other Aussie BBQ books.

Garry Egger
Scientific Director
GutBusters

GUTBUSTER BASICS

In the *GutBuster Waist Loss Guide*, we outlined four basic principles for effective waist loss. These are as follows:

1. Changing habits
2. Moving more
3. Eating differently (particularly less fat and more fibre)
4. Trading off (food and drink for exercise)

We'll summarise each of these for those who may not be aware of them.

1. CHANGING HABITS

Habits are ways of responding that become automatic and allow us to do and think about other things while we're doing them. Habits form from a connection between a stimulus and a response. That stimulus is not always hunger but can be a cue that we've learned to associate with eating. For example, an advertisement during a television program can come to be associated with getting up and finding something to eat or drink. It's the advertisement, not the hunger, that leads to excessive eating.

Tips for changing habits

To break the 'habit cycle', the stimulus–response connection must be broken. There are many ways of doing this:

- Identify triggers for eating
- Measure waist size weekly and record it
- Focus on your behaviour rather than your weight
- Don't keep high-fat snack foods, chocolates, chips, biscuits, etc. in the house
- NEVER shop while hungry
- Confine eating to one place in the house (such as the dining room table)
- Leave the table immediately after eating
- Don't associate anything else, such as reading or TV, with eating
- Wait for five minutes in the middle of a meal before eating more
- Don't have peanuts or chips in the house
- Don't get into a 'shout'
- Substitute an alternative for eating, like going for a walk or washing the car
- Combine water/mineral water chasers with alcohol
- Reward yourself for *doing* things, not just *achieving* things

2. MOVING MORE

Most fat control programs emphasise diet. But more and more people are beginning to recognise the importance of movement, or exercise. The first point to make about exercise for fatness is that it's not necessarily the same as exercising for fitness. In fact, exercise is the wrong term. All you need is more movement. Movement of any kind uses up energy. And energy, as we know, if not taken in the form of food, is taken out of the body in the form of fat.

A planned exercise or fitness program will obviously burn fat, but you don't have to go to a gym or take up aerobics, or even pound the pavement in a pair of joggers. Moving more could simply mean walking a bit more instead of going everywhere in the car, getting a little more active with the kids, or mowing the lawn instead of paying someone else to do it.

Tips for moving more

Let's forget 'bust-a-gut exercise' and think about moving more, in big ways and little ways, and all the time throughout the day.

- Try to walk every day (at least six days a week) for at least 3–4 km
- Park away from a restaurant or shop or work and walk to and from
- Go for a walk or drink water instead of automatically snacking
- Have an alternative exercise planned for cold/wet days

- Organise a friend or partner to exercise with you so you can't renege
- If injury stops you walking, try a bike, swimming, a mini-tramp—anything
- Don't do any organised exercise you don't like for longer than two weeks
- Exercise BEFORE a main meal—with the exception of swimming, it reduces the appetite
- Vary your exercise (either different exercises each day or a different route each day)
- Plan ahead, and make sure you don't miss out on moving on at least two consecutive days
- Don't use a lift or escalator when you can use the stairs
- Don't ride when you can walk

3. EATING DIFFERENTLY

Losing fat doesn't necessarily mean eating less. It can mean eating differently. In particular, it means decreasing fat in the diet, and increasing fibre.

Decreasing fat in the diet

One gram of fat provides your body with 9 calories, whereas a gram of either carbohydrate or protein has only 4 calories. So fat is more fattening. It also seems to be more addictive, so the more fat we eat, the more we crave it. You can reduce fat, and hence the craving for fat and food in the following ways:

- Trim all fat off meat
- Remove skin from chicken
- Choose fish or seafood
- Buy lean meat and poultry, e.g. skinless chicken legs, breasts or thighs
- Cook with less fat by grilling, microwaving, dry frying, barbecuing or steaming
- Choose low-fat cheeses (cottage or ricotta) or reduced-fat cheeses
- Use spreads thinly—or skip them altogether
- Buy low-fat dairy products—skim or lite milk and low-fat yoghurt
- Keep to a minimum cakes, biscuits, pies, pastry, toasted muesli

Increasing fibre

Dietary fibre, which comes in plant foods, tends to create a 'full' feeling so you feel satisfied. High-fibre foods are rarely fattening, mainly because they are so bulky it is difficult to eat too much of them.

Hints for adding fibre to your diet:

- Use wholemeal bread
- Choose wholegrain cereals such as wholemeal pasta, brown rice, wholegrain crispbread, rolled oats, and wheat, barley or oat breakfast cereals
- Eat the skins of fruits and vegetables where appropriate

- Eat more vegetables and fruit
- Eat more dried peas, beans and lentils (e.g. soy beans, kidney beans, baked beans, Lima beans)
- Eat fibre with protein (a chicken and salad sandwich—not just chicken)

Decreasing fat and increasing fibre are the two main changes that can help in the early stages of a fat loss program. Sugars, although given great importance in many programs, really only need to be considered once fats are under control, and you're still not losing weight.

4. TRADING OFF

The idea of not being able to enjoy a drink stops many men trying to reduce their gut. There's good reason for alcohol being associated with weight. Every gram is equivalent to 7 calories (water has no calories). Alcohol also tends to slow down the rate fat is burned in the body because it is more easily converted to usable energy. And because it doesn't take much energy to convert fat in the blood to storage fat, the effects of alcohol can mean even more fat gets deposited on the belly. So instead of fat in the diet being used as energy, it fills the fat cell reservoirs around the waist.

Fortunately, you don't have to give up all the good things in life. What's the point in making your life miserable? You *can* enjoy a drink *and* lose weight— but to be able to do so, you'll need to make some trade-offs in the type of food you eat and the amount of exercise you do. As a rough guide, one middy of beer is roughly equal to walking or jogging about 1.5 kilometres (about a mile), although the effect of exercise on metabolic rate may reduce this distance slightly. We can say that you need to do one extra kilometre of walking for every alcoholic drink. It's a small price to pay. Alternatively, a middy of beer is equivalent to a couple of biscuits or a small piece of cake. To balance out up to 4 beers a day, you can decrease the amount of biscuits, cake or other fatty foods you eat, or increase your walking.

Trading off is a simple way of not having to drastically alter your lifestyle AND having a big effect on waist reduction. With the recipes in this book, however, you don't even have to worry about that. They're all low-fat anyway!

CAJUN LAMB CUTLETS

(serves 4)

8 well-trimmed French lamb cutlets
2 button squash, sliced
2 large button mushrooms, sliced
4 broccoli florets
1 medium carrot, sliced diagonally
1/2 capsicum, cut into thin strips
balsamic vinegar

Marinade paste
100 g natural low-fat yoghurt
4 heaped teaspoons MasterFoods Cajun Flavour Base

Keep upright
It may not sound too important, but staying on your feet, instead of sitting down while at the barbie, is going to help burn some extra energy, and hence fat (off you, not your food). Standing is always more energetic than sitting and walking more than standing. In line with 'regarding movement as an opportunity, not an inconvenience', in this case you don't even need to move.

1. Blend yoghurt and Cajun Flavour Base in a bowl.
2. Brush marinade paste on both sides of the cutlets and place onto a hot grill. Cook for 4–5 minutes until golden brown and then turn and cook for a further 3–4 minutes.
3. Place mushrooms and capsicum onto the hotplate, drizzle over balsamic vinegar and stir-fry for 3–4 minutes.

Fat ~ 6.7 g/serve

AFTER ONE OR TWO EARLY MISTAKES GOD EVENTUALLY MADE MAN IN HIS OWN IMAGE AND WAS PLEASED.

CHARGRILLED CHICKEN WITH MANGO SALAD
(serves 4)

500 g chicken breast fillets cubed, divided into 12 portions and placed on skewers
4 cups cooked Basmati rice

Marinade paste
1 orange peeled, seeded and pureed
2 teaspoons chopped coriander
2 tablespoons thick soy marinade
50 g low-fat natural yoghurt

Salad
½ salad onion, thinly sliced
½ red capsicum, sliced
1 roma tomato, diced
8 asparagus spears
2 mangoes, peeled and cubed

1. Blend marinade ingredients together in a bowl.
2. Marinate chicken skewers in marinade paste for one hour (refrigerated). Drain and reserve marinade.
3. Place chicken skewers onto a hot grill and cook for 3–4 minutes, brush with marinade and then turn and cook for a further 3–4 minutes or until golden brown.
4. Pack rice into a cup or small mould to give it shape and turn out onto each plate.
5. Arrange skewers over rice and decorate with diced tomato, capsicum and mango and finally, asparagus spears.

Fat ~ 3.6 g/serve

BIG FRANK DALEY HAD A REPUTATION AROUND TOWN FOR PERSISTANCE.

ASIAN LAMB SALAD
(serves 4)

400 g lean lamb rib fillets
cos lettuce leaves
mignonette lettuce leaves
1 Spanish onion, peeled and thinly sliced
100 g button mushrooms, sliced
8 fresh asparagus spears, blanched
1/2 capsicum, thinly sliced

Thai marinade paste
1 dessertspoon sweet chilli sauce
1 teaspoon crushed garlic
juice of 1/2 lime
juice of 1/2 lemon
1 teaspoon soft brown sugar
1 tablespoon soy sauce
1 teaspoon Thai fish sauce
100g low-fat natural yoghurt

Dressing
50 ml white wine
juice of 2 limes
1 teaspoon sweet chilli sauce
salt to season

1. Blend all marinade ingredients except yoghurt, and marinate lamb overnight.
2. Pour off marinade and blend with the yoghurt.
3. Brush paste on one side of lamb, place on hot grill and cook for 3–4 minutes. Brush paste onto top side of lamb, turn and cook for a further 3–4 minutes, continuing to baste meat. Set aside for 3–4 minutes then slice thinly.
4. Tear lettuce leaves and arrange on plates. Add mushrooms, onion and capsicum, then the sliced lamb and asparagus spears.
5. Whisk dressing ingredients together, drizzle over salad and serve.

Fat ~ 4.6 g/serve

WHERE'S WALLY?
(THE MYOPIC VERSION)

AUSSIE BEEF SALAD
(serves 4)

400 g lean beef fillet
cos lettuce leaves
mignonette lettuce leaves
1/4 medium red capsicum, cut into fine strips
24 snow pea sprouts
1/2 punnet cherry tomatoes
100 g mushrooms, sliced
1/2 Lebanese cucumber, cut into thin strips

1 carrot, shaved lengthwise into
  long curls (use a vegetable
  peeler)

Marinade paste
2 tablespoons BBQ marinade
  soy sauce
2 cloves garlic, crushed
1 dessertspoon hot sauce
tomato paste
150 g low-fat natural yoghurt

1. Brush one side of the fillet with marinade sauce and place this face down onto hot BBQ plate, then brush upper side with marinade sauce.
2. Cook for 5–6 minutes or until nicely browned, then turn and cook for a similar time until nicely browned.
3. Let stand for 5 minutes before slicing thinly into strips.
4. Arrange a combination of cos and mignonette lettuce leaves on 4 plates.
5. Arrange the tomatoes, cucumber and mushrooms on the lettuce.
6. Add the thinly sliced beef and carrot curls.
7. Decorate with strips of red capsicum and a few snow pea sprouts.

Fat ~ 4.9 g/serve

"WHEN I SAID I'D LIKE TO SEE IT AGAIN I WAS THINKING MORE IN TERMS OF A DIET."

SEAFOOD SALAD
(serves 4)

8 scallops
8 shelled prawns (leave tail end intact)
240 g salmon fillets (4 pieces)
mignonette lettuce
1 medium red capsicum
1 medium yellow capsicum
8 fresh asparagus spears, blanched
1/2 medium avocado
4 button mushrooms, sliced

Marinade
juice of 2 lemons
juice of 2 limes
2 tablespoons freshly
    chopped coriander
1 teaspoon fresh ginger

Dressing
50 ml white wine vinegar
10 ml olive oil
50 ml lemon juice
salt and pepper to taste

1. Marinate all seafood in lemon and lime juice, coriander and ginger, along with a dash of salt and pepper for 2 hours.
2. Place seafood onto a hot BBQ grill and drizzle over marinade.
3. Cook for approximately 2 minutes and then turn. Drizzle over more marinade and cook for a further 2–3 minutes.
4. Arrange 3–4 lettuce leaves on each plate.
5. Arrange prawns, scallops and salmon over lettuce.
6. Decorate with capsicum, mushrooms, asparagus and avocado.
7. Drizzle over dressing and serve immediately.

Fat ~ 6.2 g/serve

SEXUAL ORGAN HARASSMENT

CHILLI PRAWN SALAD
(serves 4)

mignonette lettuce leaves
cos lettuce leaves
20 green prawns, shelled and deveined
1 teaspoon minced ginger
$1/4$ teaspoon turmeric
1 teaspoon paprika
1 dessertspoon sweet chilli powder
2 pieces lemon grass
juice of 1 lemon
salt to taste
1 teaspoon olive oil

1. Heat the oil in a pan. Place ginger, turmeric, paprika, chilli powder and lemon grass in the hot pan and stir.
2. Add green prawns and toss everything briefly until cooked.
3. Add lemon juice, season with salt and serve immediately on a medley of lettuce, with wedges of lime and cherry tomatoes.

Fat ~ 2 g/serve

WHY THE MIXED TUG O' WAR BETWEEN THE SPOONERISTS AND THE DYSLEXIC ASSOC. ALWAYS ENDS IN A SHAMBLES.

APPLE AND ASPARAGUS SALAD

(serves 4)

mignonette lettuce (washed)
1 bunch asparagus, blanched
10–15 snow pea sprouts
1 red salad onion, peeled and sliced
2 Granny Smith apples, cored and sliced
   (sprinkle with lemon juice)

Dressing
juice of 1 lemon
juice of 1 orange
50 ml white wine vinegar
salt and pepper
2 tablespoons chopped coriander

1. Place washed lettuce leaves in a medium-sized salad bowl.
2. Layer sliced apple and onion over lettuce and decorate with asparagus and a sprinkle of snow pea sprouts.
3. Place all salad dressing ingredients in a bowl and whisk thoroughly.
4. Drizzle dressing over salad and serve.

Fat ~ 0.3 g/serve

THE UNRECOGNISED LINK BETWEEN ALZHEIMERS DISEASE AND OBESITY.

TROPICAL PORK KEBABS
(serves 4)

400 g pork fillets, cubed
4 slices fresh pineapple, cut into pieces
1 red capsicum, cut into square pieces
6 button mushrooms, cut into quarters
2 cups cooked Basmati rice

Marinade
1 tablespoon soy sauce
1 tablespoon honey

1 tablespoon sherry
1 teaspoon minced ginger
1 teaspoon hot sauce
2 cloves garlic, crushed

Mango and tomato salsa
1 mango, flesh diced
1/2 salad onion, diced
1 ripe tomato, diced

1. Place blended marinade ingredients in a plastic bag with the pork. Remove all the air from the bag, fasten with a rubber band and refrigerate overnight.
2. Fold all salsa ingredients together and refrigerate until serving.
3. Divide pork, mushrooms, capsicum and pineapple into 12 even groups and thread onto 12 soaked bamboo skewers, alternating ingredients. Barbecue kebabs over a high heat, turning after 2 minutes.
4. Pork is cooked when it feels firm and is no longer pink in the centre.
5. Serve with 1 cup cooked rice and mango and tomato salsa.

Fat ~ 2.8 g/serve

WHY WOMEN WOULD NOT EXIST IF ADAM WAS CREATED TODAY

MIXED TAPAS

(serves 4)

120 g kangaroo steak, cut in long slivers
cracked pepper
120 g chicken breast, cubed
2 dessertspoons soy marinade
50 g low-fat natural yoghurt
8 medium prawns, shelled, leaving tails intact
2 dessertspoons sweet chilli sauce
100 g low-fat natural yoghurt

Get them to do it themselves
In line with our last tip, there's often an expectation among kids that everything will be given to them by their parents. Kids currently also have a weight problem. So instead of taking their dinner and other things to them, ask them to come and get it themselves. It won't help your belly, but it may stop them from getting one.

1. Take slivers of kangaroo and arrange in folds at one end of 4 kebab skewers.
2. Roll in cracked pepper.
3. Take cubed chicken breast and arrange at one end of 4 kebab skewers.
4. Brush with soy basting marinade (soy marinade mixed with 50 g yoghurt).
5. Skewer each prawn onto a kebab skewer, tail first.
6. Brush with chilli paste (sweet chilli sauce mixed with 100 g yoghurt).
7. Place kangaroo and chicken on BBQ grill for 3 minutes, then add the prawns and cook for a further 5 minutes, turning all skewers twice.
8. Serve arranged on a platter, with salad greens and fruit chutney.

Fat ~ 2.8 g/serve

AFTER HE SOLVED HAWKING'S EQUATION OF MATTER,
SPIROS GAVE UP BODYBUILDING.

PESTO-CRUSTED LAMB FILLET

WITH A BROWN MUSHROOM SAUCE, SERVED ON POTATO MASH AND A MEDLEY OF VEGETABLES

(serves 4)

2 x 200 g Lean Lamb rumps
2 dessertspoons pinenuts
½ cup fresh basil, washed
½ cup fresh parsley
juice of 1 lemon

2 cloves garlic, crushed
1 teaspoon Worcestershire sauce
2 slices fresh wholemeal bread, crusts removed and cut into small pieces
canola oil spray

1. Place pinenuts in a food processor on high until the pinenuts resemble coarse breadcrumbs and set aside.
2. Take the basil, parsley, garlic and lemon juice and process into a coarse paste.
3. Add pinenuts, Worcestershire sauce and bread and process pesto into a smooth paste.
4. Spray the BBQ plate lightly with canola oil, brown meat on both sides.
5. Smear pesto over the top sides of lamb rumps.
6. Place meat over the grill in an oven-style BBQ and close the lid.
7. Cook on high heat for 25 minutes for medium-rare or 30 minutes for medium.
8. Open lid and cook for a further 5–10 minutes. (*More instructions overleaf*)

9. Slice each lamb rump into 6–8 thick slices.
10. Divide potato mash into 4, and create a small mound in the centre of each of the 4 serving plates.
11. Place 3–4 slices of lamb in a layered fashion over the potato mash.
12. Dress with mushroom sauce and decorate with a sprig of basil and slivers of red capsicum.
13. Serve with a medley of vegetables.

Fat ~ 1.6 g/serve

MUSHROOM SAUCE

4 shallots, chopped
1 cup red wine
1 cup beef stock
100 g small field mushrooms
2 cloves garlic, crushed

1 teaspoon olive oil
cracked pepper
1 tablespoon thyme leaves

1. Place shallots, garlic and olive oil into a pan and cook for 1 minute.
2. Add mushrooms to the pan and cook for 1 minute.
3. Add stock, wine, thyme and pepper to pan and allow to simmer until mushrooms are soft and sauce has reduced by half.

22

POTATO MASH

4 medium white potatoes, peeled
150–200 ml skim milk
salt and pepper to taste

1. Cut potato into chunks and cook in the microwave for 8 minutes on high.
2. Place cooked potato and milk into a food processor and blend to a smooth thick consistency. Season with salt and pepper.

MEDLEY OF VEGETABLES

corn-on-the-cob wheels
carrot buttons
broccoli florets

1. Take 2 cobs of corn and cut them into 1 cm thick cob wheels.
2. Take 2 large carrots and cut into 5 cm long buttons.
3. Take 1 medium head of broccoli and cut into 8 florets.
4. Place all vegetables into a microwave-proof dish and cook on high for 6–7 minutes.

Fat ~ 9.7 g/serve

STEPMASTER

LIME COCONUT-SCENTED OCEAN TROUT CUTLETS
(serves 4)

4 ocean trout cutlets, 500 g
rocket leaves

Marinade
rind of 1 lime
1 clove garlic, crushed
1 dessertspoon sweet chilli sauce
1 x 200 ml can light evaporated milk

1 teaspoon coconut essence
1 tablespoon fish sauce
2 tablespoons coriander leaves,
  chopped

1. Mix all marinade ingredients.
2. Place trout cutlets into a shallow dish and cover with marinade. Cover and refrigerate for 1 hour.
3. Remove cutlets from marinade, place onto a hot BBQ plate and spoon over 2–3 dessertspoons of marinade. Cook for 3–4 minutes on each side. After turning the cutlets, spoon over more of the marinade.
4. Arrange some rocket leaves onto each serving plate along with mango and tomato salad.
5. Place cooked cutlets on top and decorate with wedges of mango and serve immediately.

MANGO AND TOMATO SALAD

2 mangoes, flesh cubed
1 salad onion, diced
2 teaspoons chopped coriander
2 ripe tomatoes, diced
1 lime

1. Cut mangoes lengthwise either side of the seed and cube the flesh.
2. Place all ingredients into a bowl and toss and refrigerate until serving.
3. Squeeze extra lime juice over the salad after serving.

> **Variation:** If you substitute barramundi for the ocean trout, fat is reduced to 3.6 g per serve.

Fat ~ 11 g/serve (but these are good fats from fish oils)

FAST FOOD - THE NEXT STEP.

LIME CHICKEN SALAD
(serves 4)

550 g chicken breast fillets (cut into 1 cm strips)
cos lettuce leaves
mignonette lettuce leaves
1 lime cut into 8 wedges
½ punnet cherry tomatoes, cut in half
16 snow peas
½ yellow capsicum, sliced thinly

Marinade paste
juice and rind of 2 limes
1 dessertspoon sweet chilli sauce
100 g low-fat natural yoghurt
2 teaspoons soy sauce

Dressing
juice of 2 limes
50 ml white wine vinegar
salt to taste

1. Tear lettuce into pieces and arrange onto 4 plates.
2. Arrange cherry tomatoes, snow peas, yellow capsicum and lime wedges.
3. Blend all marinade paste ingredients in a small bowl.
4. Brush liberally onto one side of the chicken fillets and place them on the grill.
5. Brush top side of chicken fillets with marinade paste and cook for 3–4 minutes or until nicely golden.
6. Turn chicken and cook for a further 3–4 minutes.
7. Once cooked, slice thinly and layer over salad.
8. Whisk all dressing ingredients together, drizzle over salad and serve.

Fat ~ 3.5 g/serve

"I can't decide whether to have the 'Special with the Lot' or the 'Weight Watchers Delight.'"

THE PERFECT STEAK
Golden rules

- Always begin cooking on a high heat to seal surfaces and then reduce heat and continue cooking.
- Do not over-turn your meat—turn no more than 3 times.
- Use tongs, not a fork, to turn meat.
- Test meat using tongs, pressing meat to identify texture.
- Marinate with wine or citrus-based marinades to aid tenderness. Best results come from marinating overnight (or for at least 2 hours) in the refrigerator.

Touch test—approximate cooking times

Rare	Springy	2–3 minutes each side
Medium	Firmer	4–6 minutes each side
Well done	Very firm	6–9 minutes each side

"Your problem is Obesus Olympus Corruptus.
I advise you to resign from the I.O.C."

FILLET STEAK
(serves 4)

500 g rib eye fillet (4 pieces)
300 ml red wine

1. Marinate steak in red wine overnight.
2. Place fillets onto a hot grill for 2 minutes and then turn, cook for 2 minutes, then reduce heat slightly and cook for a further 2–4 minutes.
3. Turn again and cook for a further 2–4 minutes.
4. Serve with a green salad and hot crusty bread.

Fat ~ 9.5 g/serve

WHY NEWTON'S LAW OF GRAVITY WOULD NEVER HAVE BEEN
DISCOVERED IF HE HAD LIVED TODAY.

VINDALOO CHICKEN AND ASIAN NOODLES
(serves 4)

700 g chicken breast fillets (cubed)
2 tablespoons Patak's Vindaloo Paste
canola oil spray
4 bricks Chang's Long Life Noodles
snow peas
1/4 cup shallots, chopped

1 teaspoon coriander and lemon
  grass paste
4 stalks fresh lemon grass, cut
  into 2 cm pieces
1/2 cup red capsicum, diced

1. Place chicken and vindaloo paste in a bowl and mix thoroughly until chicken is coated with paste.
2. Spray a hot pan lightly with canola oil.
3. Cook chicken until golden brown (5–8 minutes).
4. While chicken is cooking, place noodles in a pot of boiling water and cook for 4 1/2 minutes. Add snow peas and shallots and cook for a further 30 seconds.
5. Drain noodles and vegetables in a colander, mix through coriander and lemon grass paste.
6. Serve in 4 bowls, with vindaloo chicken placed on top.
7. Decorate with fresh lemon grass and red capsicum.

Fat ~ 8.5 g/serve

WHY THE INCIDENCE OF SHARK ATTACKS IN AUSTRALIA HAS DECREASED.

CHARGRILLED SALMON FILLETS WITH A BALSAMIC MARINADE
(serves 4)

800 g salmon fillets
150 ml balsamic vinegar
150 ml lime juice

1. Marinate salmon fillets in lime juice and vinegar for 60 minutes in the refrigerator.
2. Cook salmon fillets on a hot BBQ grill for 4–5 minutes, then turn and cook for a further 3–4 minutes. Drizzle marinade over the fillets while cooking.
3. Serve with mashed potato and green salad.

Fat ~ 10.2 g/serve (but the fat is from good fish oils only)

Forget the sugar substitutes

Sugar substitutes have been proposed for a long time to cut down total energy in a diet. However, it's well known that it is not sugar but fat that is the main culprit. It's also not quite clear whether taking a sugar substitute leads to a greater total food intake for the rest of the day, but it's quite possible. Unless you're a huge sugar eater, there's no need to worry about the sugar substitutes.

MAIN COURSES

DUCK EVOLUTION.

GRILLED BARRAMUNDI FILLETS WITH A LIME AND PESTO MARINADE

(serves 4)

800 g barramundi fillets
juice of 2 limes
2 teaspoons John West minced lemon grass
2 tablespoons Sunshine Fresh Basil Pesto
rocket lettuce
1 punnet cherry tomatoes
½ salad onion, peeled and sliced finely
20 ml balsamic vinegar

1. Marinate barramundi fillets in lime juice and lemon grass for 30 minutes.
2. Brush each fillet on both sides with the pesto paste.
3. Cook for 3–4 minutes on a hot grill plate then turn and cook for a further 3–4 minutes.
4. Wash rocket lettuce and break into small pieces.
5. Wash cherry tomatoes and cut in half.
6. Arrange rocket lettuce and tomatoes in a bowl and drizzle with balsamic vinegar.

Fat ~ 4.2 g/serve

FRED DOES FOR THE MALE GUT WHAT
LORD BYRON DID FOR THE ENGLISH
LANGUAGE.

PEPPERED LAMB FILLET WITH FRUIT CHUTNEY
(serves 4)

500 g lamb fillet
2 tablespoons freshly ground black pepper
Rosella Fruit Chutney

1. Roll fillet in freshly ground black pepper.
2. Slice fillet into four lengthways.
3. Cook on a hot grill plate for 4–5 minutes and then turn and cook for a further 4–5 minutes.
4. Serve with fruit chutney, a green salad (page 71) and sweet potato chips (page 73).

Fat ~ 5.0 g/serve

LIME AND CORIANDER SEARED CUTTLEFISH
(serves 4)

400 g cuttlefish, cleaned and cut into 1 cm/3 cm strips
juice of 2 limes
1 teaspoon of coriander and lemon grass paste
3 dessertspoons sweet chilli sauce
1 teaspoon fish sauce
1 lime rind finely grated
1 red capsicum cut into thin strips
1 avocado (sliced)

1. Blend lime juice, coriander and lemon grass paste, sweet chilli sauce, fish sauce and lime rind in a bowl.
2. Marinate cuttlefish in this blend in the refrigerator for 2 hours.
3. Place cuttlefish onto a hot BBQ plate, drizzle over marinade and cook for approximately 30 seconds, tossing cuttlefish as if stir-frying in a wok.
4. Decorate with thin strips of red capsicum, 1 slice of avocado and a wedge of lime. Serve immediately.

Fat ~ 2.0 g/serve

THE FATE THAT AWAITS GOOD LOOKING SKINNY PEOPLE ON JUDGEMENT DAY.

PORK FILLET WITH APPLE AND MUSTARD MARINADE
(serves 4)

400 g pork fillet, sliced into 1.5 cm
thick pieces
1 jar apple sauce
2 dessertspoons Dijon mustard
2 large peeled and washed sweet
potatoes, cut into large pieces
150 ml skim milk

Vegetables
1 red capsicum, seeded and cut into
strips
20 snow peas, washed
8 button mushrooms, cut into
quarters

1. Blend apple sauce and mustard in a bowl—this is the marinade.
2. Place pork fillet in a large dish, cover with marinade, refrigerate 2 hours.
3. Microwave sweet potato on high for 8 minutes, then mash it into a smooth texture and blend skim milk through the mash.
4. Remove pork fillets from the bowl and brush both sides with marinade.
5. Place pork fillets onto a hot BBQ grill and cook for 3–4 minutes. Turn pork fillet and cook for a further 3–4 minutes or until golden brown. Drizzle marinade over pork while cooking. Pork is cooked when it feels firm and is no longer pink inside.
6. Microwave capsicum, snow peas and mushrooms on high for 3–4 minutes.
7. Divide sweet potato into four and spoon onto plates, layer pork fillets on top, followed by the vegetables.

Fat ~ 5.5 g/serve

"I ALWAYS RUN OUT OF CHALK WITH THESE BIG MAC ADDICTS."

PESTO–CAJUN BEEF FILLET
(serves 4)

2 x 200 g beef fillets, sliced into 1.5 cm- thick pieces
1 tablespoon tomato paste
3 teaspoons MasterFoods Cajun seasoning powder
2 teaspoons pesto paste

1. Blend tomato paste, Cajun seasoning and pesto paste in a small bowl.
2. Brush marinade paste onto both sides of each piece of fillet and place onto a hot grill.
3. Cook for 2 minutes and then turn and cook for a further 2 minutes. Turn the heat to medium and cook for a further 2 minutes.
4. Serve with a green salad and hot crusty bread rolls.

Fat ~ 9.0 g/serve

THE LONE RANGER AND TONTO SLIGHTLY PAST THEIR PRIME.

SEEDED MUSTARD BEEF FILLET
(serves 4)

500 g rib eye fillet (4 pieces)
2 tablespoons seeded mustard

1. Brush both sides of each fillet liberally with mustard.
2. Place fillets onto a hot grill and cook for 2 minutes and then turn and cook for 2 minutes.
3. Reduce heat to a medium setting and cook for a further 2–4 minutes.
4. Serve with baked potato wedges and a Mediterranean salad.

Fat ~ 6 g/serve

PREHISTORIC AEROBICS.

TERIYAKI BEEF KEBABS
(serves 4)

400 g beef fillet, cubed
250 ml Teriyaki sauce
2 cloves garlic, crushed
8 soaked bamboo skewers
Basmati rice (enough to make 4 cups when cooked)
8 yellow button squash, cut into quarters
8 medium broccoli florets

1. Blend Teriyaki sauce and garlic in a bowl.
2. Divide beef cubes into 8 portions and thread them onto bamboo skewers.
3. Place beef kebabs into a large bowl, cover with marinade and refrigerate for 2 hours.
4. Place kebabs onto a hot grill and cook for 2–3 minutes, then cook for a further 2–3 minutes.
5. Microwave squash and broccoli on high for 4 minutes.
6. Arrange 2 beef kebabs over 1 cup of cooked Basmati rice for each person, along with button squash and broccoli, and serve.

Fat ~ 9.5 g/serve

"LOOK OUT! HE'S MOVING TOWARDS THE MIDDLE!"

PAN-FRIED WHITING FILLETS
(serves 4)

400 g whiting fillets
juice of 3 lemons
2 tablespoons white flour

1. Lightly dust whiting fillets with white flour.
2. Place fillets onto a hot BBQ plate and drizzle with lemon juice.
3. Cook for 3 minutes, or until golden brown and turn.
4. Drizzle with more lemon juice and cook for a further 1–2 minutes.
5. Serve with potato wedges and coleslaw.

Fat ~ 1.0 g/serve

QUENTIN FURLONGER WAS SO BIG HE HAD HIS OWN
WEATHER PATTERN

NEPTUNE'S BBQ MEDLEY
(serves 4)

100 g baby octopus
100 g shelled king prawns
100 g natural oysters
100 g barramundi fillets, cubed
mignonette lettuce leaves, torn into pieces
1 large mango, cubed
1 bunch asparagus spears, washed, with 2.5 cm cut off ends
juice of 1 lime

Marinade
juice of 2 limes
2 tablespoons sweet
  chilli sauce
2 teaspoons coriander
  and lemon grass paste
150 ml white wine

1. Blend lime juice, sweet chilli sauce, coriander and lemon grass paste and white wine in a bowl.
2. Place octopus, prawns, oysters and barramundi into the marinade and refrigerate for 2 hours or overnight.
3. Place seafood onto a hot BBQ plate and drizzle with marinade.
4. Cook for 3–4 minutes and then turn. Drizzle with more marinade and cook for a further 2–3 minutes.
5. Place lettuce leaves onto 4 plates and top with seafood medley, cubed mango and fresh asparagus spears.
6. Drizzle with lime juice and serve immediately.

Fat ~ 3 g/serve

THE UN RECOGNISED BENEFITS OF COMPUTER DATING

SATAY CHICKEN KEBABS
(serves 4)

600 g chicken breast fillets
4 squares of cooked Chang's Long Life
    noodles
red capsicum, diced
8 soaked bamboo skewers

Satay Sauce
2 tablespoons peanut butter

200 ml skim milk
1 tablespoon sweet chilli sauce
2 teaspoons soy sauce

Vegetable Medley
2 medium carrots, diced
2 medium zucchini, diced
8 medium broccoli florets
red capsicum, seeded and diced

1. Divide chicken into 8 portions and thread onto skewers.
2. Place peanut butter and skim milk in a saucepan, place onto a hotplate on medium heat, stirring occasionally, while the peanut butter melts and milk reduces, forming a thick consistency.
3. Stir in soy and chilli sauces and set aside.
4. Place chicken kebabs onto a hot grill and cook for 3–4 minutes and turn and cook for a further 2–3 minutes.
5. Microwave the vegetable medley on high for 4–5 minutes.
6. Divide noodles into 4 bowls, top with vegetable medley.
7. Arrange kebabs over the noodles and vegetables and top with satay sauce. Decorate with diced red capsicum and serve.

Fat ~ 8.5 g/serve

"GATFUTS" AS HIS MATES CALLED HIM, HAD NEVER EVEN HEARD
OF THE REV. ALBERT SPOONER.

TOMATO-CRUSTED PORK MEDALLIONS
(serves 4)

500 g pork medallions (4 medallions)
1 (440 g) can diced tomatoes with basil and
   onions, well drained
1 dessertspoon soy sauce
2 tablespoons tomato paste

1 teaspoon basil paste
12 baby (chat) jacket potatoes,
   washed

1. Blend diced tomatoes and soy sauce in a bowl. (Reserve 2 tablespoons of diced tomatoes.)
2. Place pork medallions into tomato and soy blend and refrigerate for 2 hours.
3. Blend tomato and basil pastes along with 2 tablespoons of diced tomatoes and brush onto pork medallions. Cook pork medallions over a high heat, turning after 3–4 minutes.
4. Cook for a further 3–4 minutes. Pork is cooked when it feels firm and is no longer pink in the centre.
5. While pork is cooking, microwave the potatoes on high for 6–8 minutes.
6. Serve pork with baby jacket potatoes and a green salad.

Fat ~ 6.5 g/serve

BRIAN RECOVERED QUICKLY WHEN HE DISCOVERED FBT WAS NOT FAT BELLY TAX.

COLESLAW
(serves 4)

2 cups cabbage, shredded
1 cup carrot, grated
1/4 cup onion, grated

Dressing
1/2 cup apple cider vinegar
1/4 cup lime juice
1/4 cup lemon juice
salt and ground pepper to taste

SIDE DISHES

1. Place all dressing ingredients into a bowl and whisk through.
2. Mix thoroughly the cabbage, carrot and onion.
3. Decorate with dressing near to serving.

Fat ~ 0

IF CROSS SPECIES BREEDING OCCURRED.

MEDITERRANEAN SALAD
(serves 6)

2 cups mignonette lettuce
2 cups cos lettuce
150 g low-fat fetta cheese
1/4 cup black olives
1 medium white onion
6 Roma tomatoes

Dressing
10 ml extra virgin olive oil
100 ml lemon juice
100 ml vinegar
salt and pepper to taste

1. Wash and separate mignonette and cos lettuce.
2. Cut fetta cheese into 1 cm cubes.
3. Peel and thinly slice onion.
4. Wash tomatoes and cut into wedges.
5. Place lettuce, onion, tomatoes, fetta cheese and olives in a small bowl and toss.
6. Place all dressing ingredients in a bowl and whisk together thoroughly.
7. Drizzle dressing over salad and serve immediately.

Fat ~ 5.8 g/serve

SIDE DISHES

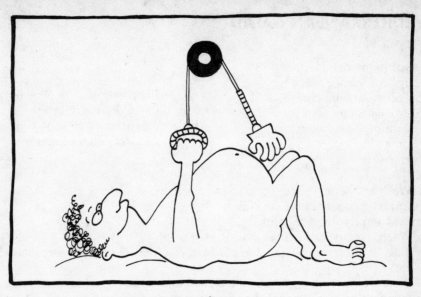

TECHNO - EROTICISM

POTATO SALAD

(serves 4)

4 medium potatoes, peeled, washed and cut
   into chunks
30 g lean eye bacon, diced
½ onion, finely diced
2 dessertspoons Kraft Free
Mayonnaise
1 dessertspoon parsley, finely chopped

Try a spicy entrée
Some spicy foods contain an ingredient known as 'capsaicin', which it is thought may help raise the metabolic rate and hence add to fat loss. Recently it's also been shown that a spicy entrée of chillies or peppers can result in a decrease in the total amount of food eaten at the main meal. If you feel like an entrée, spicy may be the way to go.

1. Cook potatoes in a microwave on high 6–8 minutes then cool, covered, in the fridge.
2. In a hot non-stick frypan, lightly brown bacon and onion.
3. Fold bacon and onion through cool potato, add the mayonnaise and fold through.
3. Decorate with chopped parsley.

Fat ~ 1.6 g/serve

SIDE DISHES

TOMATO AND BOCCONCINI SALAD
(serves 4)

8 large tomatoes
100 g bocconcini cheese
1/2 cup snow pea sprouts
1 teaspoon freshly chopped basil

Dressing
10 ml extra virgin olive oil
50 ml balsamic vinegar
salt and pepper to taste

Do it slowly

There are only two ways to eat: fast and slow. If you eat fast, the brain doesn't have time to catch up with the stomach until it begins to overflow. That way you're likely to have eaten more than you need, and because something has to be done with the excess, it's then stored as fat. Eating slowly, on the other hand, allows the brain to keep up with the mouth. That way you're less likely to over-eat.

1. Wash tomatoes and cut into thick slices.
2. Slice bocconcini cheese into 1/2 cm slices.
3. Arrange tomatoes on a flat plate and place a slice of cheese on each tomato slice.
4. Place all dressing ingredients into a bowl and whisk together thoroughly.
5. Decorate tomato salad with snow pea sprouts, sprinkle with basil, then drizzle with dressing and serve immediately.

Fat ~ 5 g/serve

SIDE DISHES

HOW ONE OF THE OTHER DEADLY SINS PUT PAID TO LUST.

ORANGE AND PINENUT SALAD
(serves 6)

2 cups mignonette lettuce
½ medium avocado
2 medium oranges
1 red onion
1 dessertspoon pinenuts
½ cup snow pea sprouts

Dressing
10 ml extra virgin olive oil
1 clove garlic, crushed
2 tablespoons balsamic vinegar
50 ml orange juice
salt and freshly ground pepper

1. Wash and separate lettuce leaves.
2. Peel and pit avocado and slice into thin wedges.
3. Using a sharp knife, remove all pith and peel from the oranges and cut into segments.
4. Peel and slice onion thinly.
5. Place pinenuts in a hot oven and roast for 5–10 minutes or until golden brown.
6. Combine all dressing ingredients into a bowl and whisk together thoroughly.
7. Arrange lettuce leaves on a flat serving plate.
8. Decorate lettuce with avocado, orange, onion and snow pea sprouts.
9. Sprinkle with roasted pinenuts.
10. Drizzle dressing over and serve immediately.

Fat ~ 7 g/serve

JONAH'S BROTHER WARREN WHO GOT REVENGE
BY SWALLOWING A WHALE WHOLE.

GREEN SALAD
(serves 4)

cos lettuce, torn into pieces
6 Roma tomatoes, cut into wedges
cucumber, sliced
salad onion, peeled and sliced

Dressing
40 ml lemon juice
5 ml olive oil
salt and pepper to taste

Put your dog on a weight loss program
It's not surprising that there's a correlation between overweight dogs and overweight masters. And while many masters may not be concerned about themselves, they would like to do the right thing by Fido. Interestingly, once you start taking the dog for a walk and giving him less fatty scraps, Fido will start to thin down. (Strangely, so will you.)

1. Place all salad ingredients into a bowl and toss.
2. Place lemon juice, salt, pepper and olive oil in a sealed container and shake to blend ingredients.
3. Drizzle over salad and serve immediately.

Fat ~ 1.1 g/serve

GOD TAKES GLUTTONY OFF THE LIST OF SEVEN DEADLY SINS IN ORDER TO ASSIST SATAN WITH HIS ACCOMMODATION PROBLEM.

SWEET POTATO CHIPS
(serves 4)

2 sweet potatoes
canola oil spray

1. Preheat oven to 180°C.
2. Wash sweet potatoes and cut into thick chips.
3. Microwave sweet potatoes for 8 minutes.
4. Place potato pieces on a baking tray lined with GladBake.
5. Spray with canola oil spray and bake in preheated oven for 30 minutes.

Fat ~ 8.70 g/serve

Beware the drinker's trap

As you know from the GutBuster program, alcohol per se is not fattening. It's what you have with it that causes a 'beer plus fat' gut, rather than a 'beer gut' alone. But alcohol with a meal tends to encourage a greater total intake of food (particularly fat). Unless you are aware of this, you won't get the advantages of the 'beer' without the 'gut'. Be especially wary of total food intake with alcohol.

"Here am I, fit, virile, the product of a healthy lifestyle and multiple vitamin supplements..."

"... while there you are, fat and flabby with solar keratosis and a smokers breath that would kill a cane toad."

"So tell me, where did Darwin say my phenotype would languish anxiously, lonely and sexually unrequited..."

"... while yours would be progenerated through the genes of countless maidens of untold beauty"

I DUNNO, SEEYA.

SPINACH AND RASPBERRY SALAD
(serves 4)

1 bunch of spinach, washed and shredded
1 punnet of fresh raspberries
1 tablespoon pinenuts
$\frac{1}{2}$ cup white wine vinegar
juice of 1 orange

1. Place shredded spinach into a bowl and microwave on high for 30 seconds, then refrigerate for 1 hour to chill.
2. Place the chilled shredded spinach on a serving plate and sprinkle with raspberries and pinenuts.
3. Mix white wine vinegar and orange juice together, drizzle over spinach and serve immediately.

Fat ~ 1.3 g /serve

WHY ONLY BIG BELLIED MEN SHOULD BE ABLE
TO RUN FOR THE PRESIDENCY.

BAKED POTATO WEDGES
(serves 4)

4 medium white potatoes, washed and cut
    into wedges
1 egg white, beaten

1. Pre-heat the oven to 180°C.
2. Place egg white and potato wedges into a
   plastic bag and seal with an elastic band.
   Shake bag, covering all wedges with egg
   white.
3. Place wedges onto a tray covered with Glad Bake.
4. Bake in the oven for 30–40 minutes, until golden brown.

Fat ~ 0.2 g/serve

> ### Go for a 'fat chip'
> Chips are made from potatoes, which inherently have negligible fat. It's only when the chips are cooked in oil that they soak up fat. The 'thinner' the chip the more oil it is likely to soak up and hence the more fattening it is likely to become. The best chip therefore is a thick chip which is fat only in size, rather than in the fat it contains.

SIDE DISHES

"NO MORE FAT JOKES. RIGHT?"

MEDLEY OF CHARGRILLED VEGETABLES
(serves 4)

1 red capsicum, seeded and cut into quarters
1 yellow capsicum, seeded and cut into quarters
2 medium tomatoes, cut into halves
1 eggplant, sliced into 1 cm thick pieces
canola oil spray

1. Microwave eggplant on high for 6 minutes.
2. Microwave capsicum on high for 4 minutes.
3. Microwave tomatoes on high for 3 minutes.
4. Lightly spray all vegetables with canola oil.
5. Place vegetables onto a hot grill and cook for 1–2 minutes and then turn.
6. Cook for a further 1–2 minutes and then serve.

Fat ~ 0.3 g/serve

SIDE DISHES